D1406142

## DATE DUE

# ROMANIA

# MAJOR WORLD NATIONS
# ROMANIA

Julian Popescu

## CHELSEA HOUSE PUBLISHERS
### Philadelphia

**Chelsea House Publishers**

Copyright © 2000 by Chelsea House Publishers,
a division of Main Line Book Co.
All rights reserved.
Printed in Malaysia

First Printing.

1 3 5 7 9 8 6 4 2

Library of Congress Cataloging-in-Publication Data

Popescu, Julian.
[Let's visit Romania]
Romania / Julian Popescu.
p.   cm. — (Major world nations)
Includes index.
Summary: An introduction to the geography, history, economy,
government, culture, and people of the second largest country in
south-eastern Europe.
ISBN 0-7910-5396-2 (hc)
1. Romania—Juvenile literature.  [1. Romania.]  I. Series.
DR205.P58   1999
949.8—dc21        99-13406
CIP

ACKNOWLEDGEMENTS

The Author and Publishers are grateful to the following organizations and individuals
for permission to reproduce copyright photographs in this book:
Camera Press Ltd; Barnaby's Picture Library; J Allan Cash;
Paul Popper Ltd; Mrs. Eileen Preston and the Romanian Embassy.

# CONTENTS

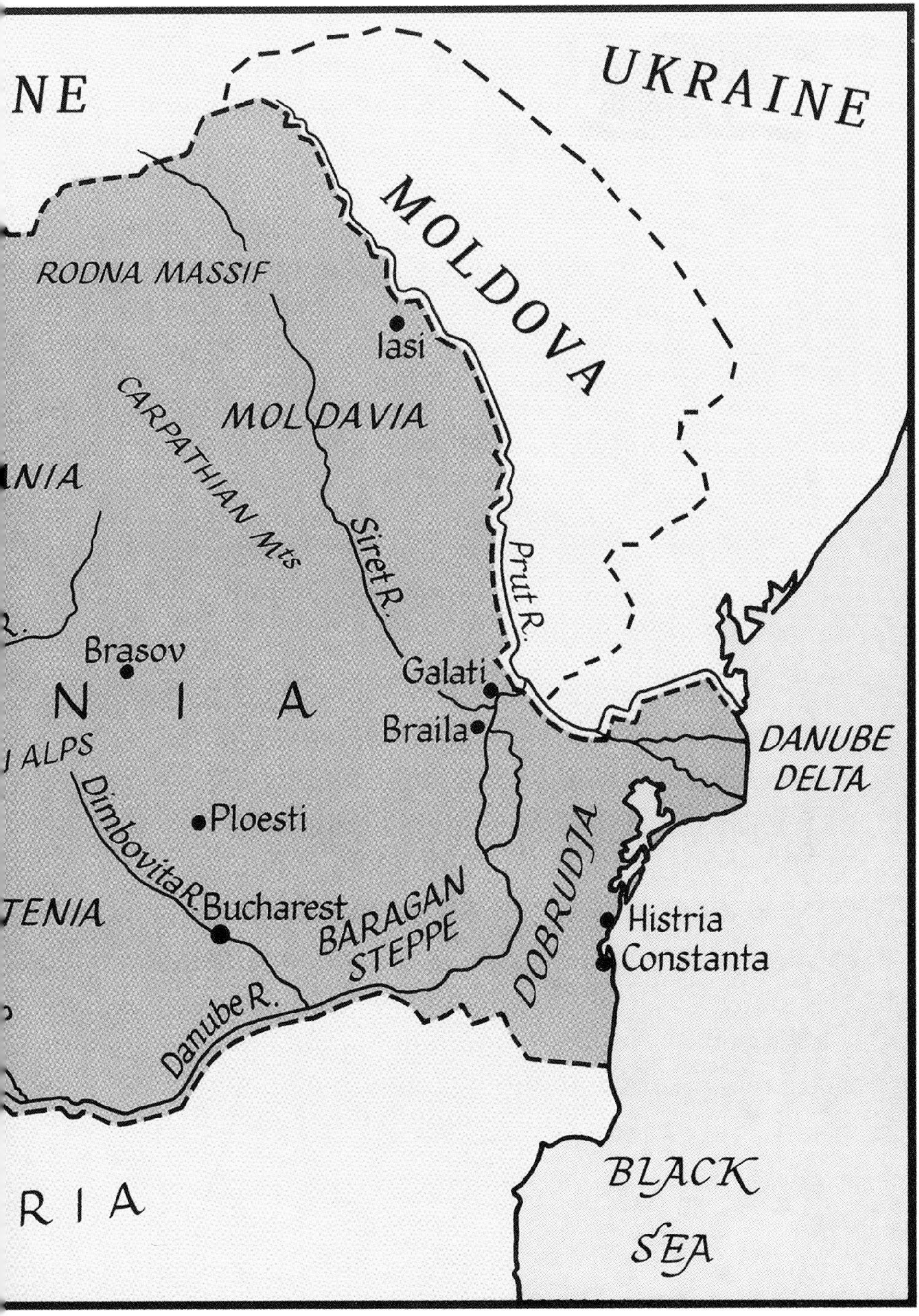

NE

UKRAINE

MOLDOVA

*RODNA MASSIF*

Iasi

*MOL DAVIA*

*CARPATHIAN Mts*

NIA

Siret R.

Prut R.

Brasov

Galati

ANIA

Braila

*DANUBE
DELTA*

ALPS

Ploesti

*Dimbovita R.*

Bucharest

*BARAGAN
STEPPE*

*DOBRUDJA*

Histria

TENIA

Constanta

Danube R.

BLACK

RIA

SEA

# FACTS AT A GLANCE

## Land and People

| | |
|---|---|
| **Official Name** | Romania |
| **Location** | On the Balkan peninsula in southeastern Europe |
| **Area** | 91,670 square miles (237,500 square kilometers) |
| **Climate** | Temperate |
| **Capital** | Bucharest |
| **Other Cities** | Constanta, Iasi, Timisoara, Galati |
| **Population** | 23 million |
| **Population Distribution** | Urban, 55.4 percent; rural, 44.6 percent |
| **Major Rivers** | Danube, Siret, Prut, Olt, Mures |
| **Mountains** | Carpathian, Transylvanian Alps, Apuseni, Rodna Massif |
| **Highest Point** | Mount Moldoveanu, 8,343 feet (2,542 meters) |
| **Official Language** | Romanian |
| **Other Languages** | Hungarian, German |

8

| | |
|---|---|
| **Ethnic Groups** | Romanian, 89.4 percent; Hungarian 7.1 percent |
| **Religions** | Romanian Orthodox, 70 percent; Roman Catholic, 6 percent |
| **Literacy Rate** | 97 percent |
| **Average Life Expectancy** | Males, 69.3 years; females, 75.4 years |

## Economy

| | |
|---|---|
| **Natural Resources** | Anthracite, coal, natural gas, iron, timber |
| **Division of Labor Force** | Agriculture, 34.4 percent; industry, 28.6 percent; trade, 10.4 percent |
| **Agricultural Products** | Corn, wheat, sugar beet, tobacco, hemp, potatoes, grapes, livestock |
| **Industries** | Mining, petroleum refining, food processing, iron and steel |
| **Major Imports** | Fuels, food, machinery and transportation equipment, textiles, chemicals |
| **Major Exports** | Machinery, mineral products, footwear, wine |
| **Currency** | Lei |

## Government

| | |
|---|---|
| **Form of Government** | Unitary republic |
| **Government Bodies** | National Assembly consisting of the Senate and Assembly of Deputies; Council of Ministers |
| **Formal Head of State** | President |
| **Head of Government** | Prime minister |
| **Voting Rights** | Citizens 18 years of age and older |

9

# HISTORY AT A GLANCE

| | |
|---|---|
| **600 B.C.** | Greek traders come from the south and establish trading posts and cities on the Black Sea coast. They find settlements of farmers and craftsmen already there. |
| **4th century B.C.** | The Dacians, living in the Carpathian mountains and the area called Transylvania, unite with those people living on the Black Sea to form a joint territory. |
| **101-106 A.D.** | Roman emperor Trajan leads campaigns against the Dacians and the conquered lands become a province of the Roman Empire. |
| **106-270 A.D.** | Roman colonists settle in Dacia. They build towns, roads, bridges, and aqueducts. Many Roman soldiers intermarry with the Dacians and settle in the area. |
| **late 3rd century** | Goths from the north invade the Dacian territories forcing the Roman soldiers to abandon the area and the Dacian people. Some Dacians follow the Romans when they leave and some escape to the Carpathian mountains. |
| **4th-11th centuries** | The period of the Dark Ages sees the land of the Dacians invaded by numerous groups including |

10

the Huns, Visigoths, Slavs, Bulgars, and Magyars.

**10th century** Eastern Orthodox Christianity is introduced into the area.

**11th century** The area called Transylvania is taken over by the Hungarian Empire.

**14th century** The Romanian provinces of Walachia and Moldavia are established. Along with Transylvania they will form the future country of Romania.

**15th-19th centuries** Romania is invaded by the Turkish Ottoman Empire. Romanian princes and their armies wage fierce battles against them. Eventually a truce is signed making the provinces of Walachia and Moldavia Turkish protectorates. Under Turkish rule the Romanian people are treated as serfs–forced to work for the Turkish landowners. The province of Transylvania remains part of the Austro-Hungarian Empire but its people are also treated badly.

**early 19th century** The Romanian leaders of Moldavia and Walachia seek help from the Russians to fight off their Turkish rulers. The Russians agree and eventually sign a treaty with the Turks giving these two provinces semi-independence in 1829.

**1853-1856** The Crimean War is fought against the Russian's attempts to take over the Turkish empire. In the treaty signed in 1856 the Romanian provinces of Moldavia and Walachia become united as a free state.

**1861** The new state formed after the Crimean War is officially named Romania and Bucharest is made its capital city. Alexandru Cuza becomes the first head of state.

**1881** The Romanians decide to become a monarchy and choose as their first king a German prince. He is crowned King Carol I.

**1916-1918** Romania enters World War I on the side of the Allies. The German army invades and occupies Romania for the remainder of the war.

**1919** At the end of the war the province of Transylvania is made a part of Romania.

**1940** The Soviet Union annexes the eastern part of the province of Moldavia called Bessarabia. The Romanian government joins World War II on the side of Germany and Italy.

**1944** Romania is invaded by the Russian army towards the end of the war and the Romanians join with the Russian forces to defeat the Germans.

**1947-1948** The Romanian king is forced to abdicate the throne when the communists take over the country declaring it the Romanian People's Republic.

**1950s** The communist government nationalizes all businesses and farms. It joins alliances of other communist countries including the Warsaw Pact. Industrialization is emphasized at the expense of the needs of the citizens.

**1952** Gheorghe Gheorghui-Dej becomes the communist leader of Romania.

**1960s** Relations between the Romanian government and the Soviet Union become strained as Romania tries its own innovations in communism and reaches out to the western countries of Europe.

Gheorghui-Dej makes a declaration of independence from the Soviet Union in 1964.

**1965-1989** Nicolae Ceausescu succeeds Gheorghui-Dej as leader of Romania. The Communist Party intensifies its control of the country and Ceausescu gains absolute power turning Romania into a police state. Free speech and dissent are openly suppressed. The economy collapses and bread lines, food shortages, and empty store shelves become the norm.

**1989** In December demonstrations in the city of Timisoara quickly escalate and the Communist government is overthrown in a violent revolution. Ceausescu is arrested, tried, and executed.

**1990s** Ion Iliescu becomes president of Romania in the first free multiparty elections. Disagreements arise over the course of the new government. The economy continues to suffer after years of neglect and oppression and the change to a free-market economy is a difficult one.

**1991** A new constitution is approved in December providing for a two house parliament.

**1995-1996** Romania submits its application to become a member of the European Union (EU) and the North Atlantic Treaty Organization (NATO).

The Transylvanian plateau is surrounded by mountains like these.

# 1

# Land and People

Romania is the largest country on the Balkan Peninsula in south-eastern Europe. It has an area of 91,670 square miles (237,500 square kilometers) and a population of 23 million. Most of its people are of Roman origin—in fact, "Romania" means "land of the Romans." But there are also Hungarians, Germans, Serbs, Tartars, and Russians who make up the rest of the population. All Romanian citizens, whatever their creed or race, have equal rights and opportunities.

The Romanians are proud of their Roman origin. Although most of their neighbors are Slavs, and they themselves have some Slav blood, they belong to the Latin family of western Europe. The Romanian language, like French or Italian, is called a "Romance language," because it is descended from Latin. Many Romanian words resemble French or Italian words, which makes French easy for Romanian children to learn at school.

Take a look at the map of Romania in the front of this book. You will see that it is almost circular in shape. In the center of the country is a plateau called Transylvania, which means "the land beyond the forests." This plateau is surrounded by rugged mountains which have fantastic shapes. Some of the mountains resemble rock castles, while others look like slender needles. There are many lakes and streams in these mountains, with excellent fishing. But in spring, after heavy rains, the streams become raging torrents. The torrents rush down the mountainsides, forming waterfalls or cutting a deep passage in the rocks. They cause serious soil-erosion problems in many parts of the country.

Many of the mountains and higher hills are wild and uninhabited. Shepherds pasture their sheep and goats on alpine meadows in spring and summer. In the autumn, when the mountains are covered with snow, the shepherds, dressed in sheepskin coats, drive their flocks down to the meadows in the plains.

Such villages as there are up in the mountains can only be reached by packhorse or ox-drawn carts because the roads are narrow and steep. In winter people travel in sleds or on skis.

Beyond the mountains are wooded hills, which give way to vast plains. The flat and treeless plain, or *steppe* as it is called in the southeastern part of the country, is known as "Romania's granary" because so much wheat is grown there. There the weather is dry and hot during the summer. In winter, blizzards sweep in with the cold easterly winds and the roads become blocked by huge snowdrifts.

During the Second World War, Romania, like other countries of southeastern Europe, became a battlefield. There was bitter fighting between German and Russian armies. Finally the Russians

16

defeated the Germans and, with the help of the Romanians, drove the Germans out of the country. When the war ended, many towns and villages lay in ruins and food was scarce. There was famine in some parts of the country and life was hard.

Today all this has changed. New factories, shops, and blocks of apartments have been built. The towns are growing fast; and many peasants have left the land to become factory workers. Those who are left work on large cooperative farms.

Outside the towns, roads and bridges were built for the growing traffic. Rivers were dammed to produce power for transportation and new industries. Farms are using modern methods of irrigation and more and more tractors and machinery to increase production of grains, vegetables, and fruit. Oil refineries have been built in the plains north of the Danube River to process the crude oil gushing up from numerous wells.

**Romanian peasants wearing traditional clothes.**

The majority of Romanians are peasants. They work very hard and for very long hours. They love their land and do not wish to emigrate as peasants of other countries sometimes do.

Romania is an important farming country. It exports wheat, fruit, vegetables, and wine to many countries of the world.

Goods are bought and sold with money called *lei*. The word means "lions" in Romanian. The *leu*, which is the singular of *lei*, is a decimal currency. Each *leu* is worth 100 *bani*. Inflation is very high in Romania. A cup of coffee in 1998 cost about 7,000 lei; a half-mile taxi ride cost 5,000 lei.

After the Second World War, Romania became a republic; and in 1948 it signed a treaty of alliance with the Soviet Union. But this treaty ran its term, and was not been renewed. Romania was then one of the few Communist countries with an independent

**Romania exports wine to many countries of the world. This girl is helping to harvest the grapes.**

foreign policy. After the fall of communism in 1989, Romania became a democratic republic.

Romania is an isolated land, and a former outpost of the Roman Empire. Ruins of Roman towns and tombs, and traces of Roman roads can be seen in many parts of the country. The peasants still keep customs and celebrate festivals handed down from generation to generation by their Roman ancestors. There are aspects of life which have not changed for centuries; and yet Romania is very much a part of the modern world. Let us visit this country and learn more about its people and their way of life.

# 2

# Geography and Climate

Romania's neighbors to the northeast are the Ukraine and Moldova. The land frontier between Romania and these two countries stretches from the Black Sea, across mountain peaks, to the hills on the edge of the Great Hungarian Plain. As you will see from the map, Romania borders on Hungary and Serbia in the west. To the east it faces Turkey across the Black Sea. In the south it shares long stretches of the Danube River with Serbia and Bulgaria.

The Black Sea is almost an inland sea. It flows into the Sea of Marmara through the narrow Bosporus Strait, belonging to Turkey, and then into the Mediterranean Sea through the Dardanelles channel. The Black Sea is Romania's most important trade waterway.

Southeastern Romania, the land between the Danube and the Black Sea, is called Dobrudja. The center of Dobrudja is a plateau formed of ancient mountains. Granite is quarried here in large quantities. The southern tip of Dobrudja is steppeland with a hot,

**Some of the rocks in the Carpathian Mountains have been eroded over the years by wind and weather. This group is typical of the strange shapes to be seen in this area.**

dry climate. Along the coast there are saltwater lagoons and silvery beaches surrounded by pine trees.

The main mountain range in Romania is a continuation of the Carpathians, which start in the Czech Republic and stretch across the part of the Ukraine. In Romania they run from north to south and then swing sharply westward until they reach the Danube. In the north they are composed of very hard volcanic rock and granite; in the south they are of limestone, granite, and crystalline rocks. Another important range, in the north, is the Rodna Massif, whose summit is Mount Petrosu. The bare and rocky Rodna Massif has many lakes in the hollows where the rock was

21

worn away by glaciers in the distant past. In the south are the Transylvanian Alps, a belt of mountains with narrow and pointed ridges. Romania's highest peaks are found here, in the Fagaras Mountains. Mount Moldoveanu rises to 8,343 feet (2,542 meters) and nearby Mount Negoiu to 8,317 feet (2,535 meters). There is always snow and ice on these summits since the temperature remains below freezing point all year round.

Our picture shows some strangely shaped rocks in the Carpathian Mountains. These owe their appearance to the wearing effect of wind and rain. There is a local legend about one of these odd formations, a clump of rocks on a high moor that looks exactly like a hag. The story goes that a greedy old woman, clothed in 99 sheepskins, climbed the mountain to seek hidden treasure. She grew so hot as she climbed that she dropped the sheepskins one by one. When she reached the top, she was left with only a thin blouse. She was frozen to death by the icy cold wind and has remained there ever since, as hard as rock, for all to see and remember.

The Transylvanian Plateau lies in the heart of Romania. This

**A mountain lynx.**

**Brown bears like this one are still to be found in Romania's mountain regions today.**

plateau of rounded hills and broad valleys is rich in vineyards. It is bordered on the eastern and southern sides by the steep wall of the Carpathians. On the western side are the Apuseni Mountains made of granite and limestone. These mountains are famous for their natural scenery. They have been worn into deep gorges and caves by rain and wind. This type of country is known as *karst*.

Nearly two-thirds of Romania's territory is made up of mountains and hills. Vegetation is sparse on most of the mountains and high hills and only moss-like plants, junipers, and shrubs grow well, although hardy flowers such as gentians, primulas, and violets grow plentifully among the rocks. Lower down there are thick forests of spruce and fir trees. Ferns and brambles grow in forest clearings. The mountains and hills are the home of wild animals that are found hardly anywhere else in Europe. The black goat, the lynx and the brown bear live there, and the Carpathian stag roams the forests. Brown squirrels, polecats, and foxes live in the

23

valleys while wolves often attack herds of dairy cows, sheep, and goats grazing the rich Alpine pastures.

Anthracite and brown coal are mined in the mountains of Romania. There are also minerals—zinc, copper, lead, silver, and gold; and rich deposits of oil and natural gas, which have been found in the valleys of the southern and eastern Carpathian foothills.

Romania's great plains are in the west and south of the country. The flat western plain is part of the Great Hungarian Plain. It is rich farming country, producing good crops of corn, wheat, and sugar beet. The plain in the south between the mountains and the Danube River is called the Danube Plain. It is a land of gently undulating hills and fertile valleys. The average summer temperature here is 71 degrees Fahrenheit (22 degrees Celsius). The average temperature in winter is below 32 degrees Celsius (0 degrees Celsius). The earth is frozen to a depth of several inches during December, January and February, and is too hard to be plowed; so during these winter months the men carry out all their repairs and make baskets or furniture.

The plains of Romania occupy one-third of the country and the majority of the population lives there. In the far south, the plains are bordered by the Danube River, and the country on the left bank is marshy and flat. The peasants have drained stretches of the marshland, however, and planted crops of tomatoes, cucumbers, and rice. Villages and farmsteads have been built wherever the land is high enough to be protected from floods. Where the marshes are left untouched, bulrushes and reeds grow thickly.

Wild duck and geese nest among the reeds, while water rats and otters search for food on the river bank.

The plains of Romania are carefully farmed. Great fields of wheat and corn stretch for miles into the distance. The villages in this part of the country have whitewashed houses, and there are orchards and plantations of tobacco, hemp, and flax. The peasants use the silky fibers of the hemp and flax plants to make their own clothes.

Life used to be hard in the plains when there was a drought and the hot south wind (called the *austru*) blew. Nowadays, much of the land has been irrigated and more and more crops are being grown. When the crops are poor, the government helps the peasants with loans and supplies of food.

Lime trees, maples, and oaks are found almost everywhere in the plains. Willow trees and poplars grow on the banks of rivers. Where the land is not cultivated, foxes and hamsters find hiding places among the tall grasses and weeds. The most common birds of the plains are pheasants, partridges, and crows.

Now let's look at the map again. The Moldavian Plateau in northeastern Romania stretches between the Carpathian Mountains and the border Moldova. This plateau is formed of high hills with steep cliffs and narrow valleys. In the past, huge forests used to cover the plateau, but many trees were cut for timber, exposing the hillsides to rain and wind, and causing soil erosion. This means that the rainwater washed away the topsoil and left much of the hillsides barren and impossible to cultivate. Forest belts have been planted on the upper slopes to stop further erosion.

Some of the Moldavian hills are rich in sandy quartz, used for making glass. There are many quarries in these hills, which also produce granite from which paving stones are made.

Mixed farming is carried out on a large scale in the Moldavian hills. Dairy cattle and pigs are reared in quantity. In this district there are many apple and plum orchards, and vineyards famous for their wines. Bees are kept here both for their honey and to set the fruit when the trees blossom.

North of the Moldavian Plateau is a treeless, grassy plain or steppe. Here, the climate is dry. In winter, a cold wind called the *crivat* blows from Siberia, leaving snowdrifts in its wake. In summer, the *crivat* brings clouds of hot dust from the east. In spite of this, the black soil of the plain is deep and fertile, and wheat, barley, and sunflowers grow well in it.

Except for a few foxes, hamsters, and hares, hardly any wild animals live in the steppe. Of the wild birds, the most common is the bustard, which can run along the ground faster than a horse.

# 3

# The Lower Danube Basin

Romania is a land of many rivers. Its most important river and navigable waterway is the Danube, which drains all the rivers from the eastern, southern and western slopes of the Carpathian Mountains. The whole of this drainage area is called the Lower Danube Basin.

The Danube is the second longest river in Europe, after the Volga. It rises in the Black Forest in Germany, and when it reaches Romania at the foothills of the Carpathian and Balkan Mountains it has already traveled 1,100 miles (1,770 kilometers). For almost all the rest of its 650-mile (1,046-kilometer) course, the Danube forms the southern border between Romania and Serbia, and then Romania and Bulgaria. Finally, the river enters Romanian territory and empties its waters into the Black Sea through the many branches of a swampy delta.

The Danube passes through varied landscapes throughout the whole of its lower course. First it flows through a string of narrow gorges stretching for nearly 70 miles (112 kilometers). The water

A view of the Cazane Gorge.

is extremely deep and the current dangerous in places. One of these, the Cazane (or Kazan) Gorge, is noted for its most beautiful scenery. "Cazane" means "cauldrons" in Romanian, and the name was given to this particular gorge because its steep, rocky banks are curved and shaped like a cauldron. On the Romanian side of the Cazane Gorge is a winding road built nearly 19 centuries ago by Roman engineers.

Lower down the river from the Cazane Gorge are the Iron Gates Rapids. Here in 1972 Romania and Yugoslavia jointly completed a huge dam across the rapids and a hydroelectric power station producing two million kilowatts of energy. Behind the dam the waters of the Danube have formed an artificial lake, greatly improving navigation through this difficult stretch of the river.

28

Locks have been built alongside the dam to allow ships and barges to go through.

After the Iron Gates dam the Danube begins to flow more and more sluggishly. The banks here are over a mile apart. There are long islands where storks and herons nest. In spring the river floods the low-lying Romanian bank and becomes 10 miles (16 kilometers) wide in places.

When the Danube reaches the mountains of Dobrudja, it is forced to turn northward. The river divides into two branches that join and break again. There are many lakes here where people swim and sail yachts. In summer the beaches on the shores of the lakes are crowded with people sunbathing and having picnics in the shade of colored umbrellas. Also at this point in the course of the Danube, Romanian civil engineers completed in 1983 the Danube Black Sea Canal across Dobrudja. The canal makes it easier for seagoing ships to sail up and down the Danube.

Finally the Danube turns eastward and forms a delta, fanning out into several branches before reaching the Black Sea. The area covers 1,000 square miles (2,590 square kilometers). The mud

**The delta area of the Danube is vast and includes swampy areas and many islands. Here the water is covered by a carpet of waterlilies.**

and sand that the river has brought from its upper reaches are deposited here, forming banks and islands with very fertile soil. Each year the delta advances into the Black Sea.

Thick forests, reeds, and rushes grow on the islands in great profusion. Wild boar, hares, and wolves live there, while otters burrow in their banks. Wild swans and pelicans with big pouches under their bills search for food in the pools and channels among the islands where water lilies and water hemlock grow. Autumn is the best time of the year to watch wildlife in the delta, for then flocks of migratory birds from the north of Europe gather together for food and rest before journeying on to the south.

There are fishermen's villages on some of the delta islands, for the Danube is full of fish, including the valuable sturgeon. The black roe of the sturgeon is better known as caviar, and considered a great delicacy. The people of the delta also make a living from cutting reeds and rushes. These are taken to mills where they are pulped and the cellulose extracted for making into paper, cardboard, and textiles. Compressed reeds are also used for building materials such as blocks and partitioning.

The most important Romanian tributaries of the Danube are the Siret and Prut rivers, which drain the Moldavian hills and join the Danube near its delta. The Olt River also joins the Danube from the north. It rises in the eastern Carpathians from the same source as the Mures River, which flows westward across Transylvania. According to legend, the Olt and Mures rivers were two brothers. They were sent by their mother to search for their father, a woodcutter, who had disappeared in the mountains. The two brothers,

Olt and Mures, set out together. But Olt was lively and restless while Mures was slow and calm. So after a time they separated, Olt going south and Mures heading for the west. Their mother, hearing no news of them, prayed to the Lord to turn them into rivers, so uniting them again. The Lord heard her prayer. He turned them into rivers whose waters unite and mingle when they reach the sea.

# 4

# Roman Conquest and Settlement

Romania is a country with a long history. Excavations have shown the existence of human life there in the Old Stone Age. The primitive inhabitants of Romania were hunters of wild animals, and fishermen, wandering from place to place with the seasons. They used tools of stone and bone, made canoes out of tree

**The ruins of the ancient Greek city of Histria on the Black Sea coast.**

**Some of the remains of Sarmizegethusa, the ancient capital of Dacia.**

trunks, and knew how to use fire. Gradually the men learned how to grow grain, rear sheep and cattle, and make pottery. The women learned how to spin thread and weave cloth.

In the Bronze and Iron Ages permanent human settlements were established in the plains and valleys. The people began using metals for tools and ornaments. Copper and tin were mixed to produce bronze. Later, iron was used for tools and weapons.

Six centuries before the birth of Christ, Greek traders came from the south and established trading posts and cities on the Black Sea coast. The Greeks traded with the native people, who were farmers and craftsmen.

At the time of Caesar, Romania was called the Kingdom of Dacia, and was ruled by King Burebista. The Dacians were skilled metalworkers, using gold, silver, and iron that they mined in the mountains. They were well organized and had a strong army of horsemen and archers who often raided Roman towns

**Like their ancestors, the Romanian peasant women are skilled in spinning and weaving. This woman is using the traditional distaff and spindle.**

and farms across the Danube. King Burebista had his capital at Sarmizegethusa, high up in the mountains. His palace was perched on top of a hill and surrounded by fortified terraces.

The Romans knew that the Dacians were good fighters. They recruited Dacian horsemen and archers for their own legions. They even sent some of them to Britain to guard Hadrian's Wall against the attacks of the wild Picts.

Toward the end of the first century A.D. the king of Dacia was the warlike Decebalus. He led the Dacians deep into the Roman provinces of the south and west, where they ransacked towns and killed a provincial governor. The Roman Emperor Trajan decided to put an end to Dacian raids. His army crossed the Adriatic Sea and the mountains of present-day Yugoslavia and camped in the plains.

Emperor Trajan's first campaign against Dacia was in 101 A.D. He attacked from the west but neither side won a decisive victory. Trajan next made plans to attack from the south. He built a

34

long bridge across the Danube, a few miles from the Iron Gates Rapids. The bridge was supported by 20 pillars of stone and brick. The weather-beaten pillars of this bridge can still be seen when the level of the Danube is low in summer. At one end of the bridge Trajan built a fortress called Drobeta. Today the Romanian city of Turnu-Severin stands on the site of the old fortress.

Trajan moved his legions, his great catapults and his battering rams across the new bridge. After heavy fighting he defeated King Decebalus, who stabbed himself rather than fall into Roman hands. The conquered land of the Dacians became a Roman province in 106 A.D. To mark his victory, Trajan built a lofty column in Rome that bears stone carvings of the Roman battles in Dacia.

Many Roman colonists settled in Dacia. They built towns and roads. They constructed bridges and aqueducts over narrow valleys. They built an important road along the Danube through the Cazane Gorge, blasting the rock to make a passage and, where the rock was too hard, drilling holes for oak beams to support the roadway. They did much to develop the country's resources, too. Work was started again in the gold and silver mines. They also mined salt and cut timber in the mountains. Roman soldiers who were too old to fight were pensioned off. These veteran soldiers married local Dacian girls and settled on the land. The province became so prosperous that it was called Dacia Felix, which means "happy Dacia." Later the Romans divided the province of Dacia into three smaller provinces in order to make for better administration.

But Roman rule did not last for long. Thousands of barbarians from the forests of the north and the grass plains of the east began to migrate to the rich lands of Europe and the Mediterranean. These hordes of wild barbarians broke through the defenses of the Roman Empire, forcing the Roman garrisons to withdraw from Dacia across the Danube to the safety of the south. Emperor Aurelian ordered his last soldiers to leave Dacia in 272 A.D. The forsaken Roman settlers and their families found shelter in the mountains and forests.

During the Dark Ages which followed, the barbarian hordes ruled the new lands and no more was heard of the Romans in Dacia. But during this period a new people was born from the intermarrying of Romans and Dacians. They were first heard of in the 14th century, over a thousand years after the Romans had left. They were called Vlachs by their neighbors. The Vlachs were actually Romanians who lived in three separate states that had their beginnings in the three provinces of Dacia. These three states were Wallachia in the south, Moldavia in the east and Transylvania in the north.

In the Middle Ages Transylvania was conquered by the Hungarians and then became a province of the Austro-Hungarian Empire. So, at an early stage in their history the Romanians came under many different rulers. But always they longed to be united again as they had been in Roman times. We shall see in the next chapter how this was achieved.

# 5

# Union and Independence

In the 15th century the Ottoman Turks conquered Constantinople, the capital of the Byzantine Empire. Soon their armies reached the banks of the Danube and started to plunder Romanian villages and towns. The Romanian princes assembled their armies and went to meet the Turks. Fierce battles raged between Romanians and Turks in the plains and forests. The Romanians showed no mercy towards Turkish prisoners, who were often impaled on sharp stakes and left to die a slow death. The Turks were equally cruel to their captives.

At last, rather than see their lands ruined by war, the Romanian princes offered to make peace with the Turks. After lengthy haggling, the Turks accepted. The two Romanian principalities, Wallachia and Moldavia, became Turkish protectorates and were obliged to pay tribute to the Turkish treasury each year. As part of the agreement Turkish troops were stationed in various fortified towns.

During this time much of Wallachia and Moldavia was covered

**This mosque reflects part of Romania's history. Muslim Turks once invaded the country and actually took possession of two principalities.**

by forests and marshes. The peasants lived in mountain villages or in the valleys and worked on farms belonging to nobles and rich landowners called *boyars*. The peasants were treated as serfs and were not free to leave their villages. They were put to work in gangs, building bridges and repairing roads. They also had to pay heavy taxes for the upkeep of the Turkish garrisons.

Peasants living in Transylvania were no better off. They were poor and had to work long hours for Hungarian landowners. In times of war they were recruited as soldiers. The peasants rioted on several occasions over these harsh conditions. Armed with pitchforks and axes, they destroyed crops, killed the nobles, and burned down mansions. Soldiers were sent to crush the rioters who, when caught alive, were executed in public or tortured to death.

Seeing how their people suffered, some of the Romanian nobles asked the Russians for help. They knew that the Russian Empire had become an important European power. Ever since the days of Peter the Great, the aim of the Russian rulers had been to expand their territory southward and drive the Turks out of the lands they had conquered in southeastern Europe. For this reason, the Russians promised that they would help the people of Wallachia and Moldavia. Already by the turn of the 19th century, the imperial Russian army, helped by the Romanian princes, was fighting the Turks across the Danube. In 1829 the Russians signed a peace treaty with the Turks. By this treaty the Romanian principalities gained semi-independence from Turkish domination.

1853 saw the outbreak of the Crimean War, famous for the charge of the Light Brigade. It was started by Britain, France, and

**In the days when the Romanian population was comprised of peasantry and nobility the nobles lived in great mansions and castles. This castle still stands in Transylvania.**

Turkey, who wished to prevent Russia from taking over the Turkish Empire. The Russians were beaten and a peace treaty was signed in Paris in 1856. This treaty was very important for the Romanian people, because one of its clauses stipulated that the inhabitants of the two Romanian principalities should be at liberty to decide whether they wished to be united as one country. The people voted in favor of union, and the principalities were united in 1859. The first head of the new state was Alexandru Cuza. The new state was officially named Romania in 1861.

A few years later, the Romanians decided that they wished to become a monarchy. They chose a German prince, Charles of Hohenzollern, as their king. So in 1881, Prince Charles was crowned King Carol I of Romania. During his reign the country prospered and the population grew.

But there were still many Romanians living under Austro-Hungarian rule in Transylvania who wished to join Romania. Their chance came in the First World War; Britain and France asked Romania to join them in their fight against the Austro-Hungarian Empire and Germany. In return, they promised Romania and Transylvania freedom to unite after the war. So Romania entered the war on the side of the Allies in 1916, only to be defeated by the powerful German army, which occupied the whole country. But when the Allies won the war, they kept their promise to Romania; and in 1919 Transylvania was united with Romania. The union almost doubled the size of Romanian territory and the country came to be called Greater Romania.

Romania did less well in the Second World War. In 1940 the

Soviet Union invaded Romanian territory and annexed the part of Moldavia east of the Prut River called Bessarabia. That same year Adolf Hitler forced Romania to give up northern Transylvania to Hungary and southern Dobrudja to Bulgaria. In exchange, Hitler promised the Romanian government the return of Bessarabia from the Russians. So the Romanian government joined Germany and Italy in the war against the Soviet Union, Britain, and the United States. This decision was unpopular with the people and ended in great tragedy for the country.

In the summer of 1944 the Russian army reached the Romanian border, after defeating the Germans, and advanced into Romania. Seeing the plight of his people, King Michael of Romania ordered his loyal officers to arrest the members of the Romanian government and signed an armistice with the Russians and the Allies. To make amends, the Romanian army was ordered to join the Russians in fighting the Germans. So Romania recovered only northern Transylvania after the defeat of Germany. The Russians gave King Michael a medal and made him a Hero of the Soviet Union.

At the end of the Second World War the land of Romania was in ruins. The communists took over the government, King Michael left the throne and, in December 1947, Romania was proclaimed a republic.

Some Romanians, loyal to the king, fled abroad and settled in France and the United States. Most of the German population lost their jobs and land and emigrated to Austria, West Germany, or South America.

The Romanian government decided that the country must have a new emblem to replace the royal coat of arms. The emblem they chose was composed of a star at the top and two sheaves of wheat enclosing an oil derrick and a rising sun against a background of mountains. They put the emblem on the country's flag also.

In the years that followed the Second World War the Romanian government nationalized all banks, factories, and shops. Land was taken away from private owners and turned into large state-owned cooperative farms. Mines and forests became public property. Plans were laid down for the whole economic development of the country, following the example of the Soviet Union.

The government also had to deal with major foreign policy problems because of Europe's division between the Communist powers and the western powers. In 1948 Romania joined the alliance of Communist countries known as the "Cominform." A year later it joined a trading system rather like the Common Market but composed of Communist member-countries, known as the "Comecon." In 1954 Romania joined the Warsaw Pact Organization. This military alliance was controlled by the Soviet Union and was similar to the powerful defence system of the West called the North Atlantic Treaty Organization (NATO).

In 1955 Romania became a member of the United Nations; ever since it has played an active part in the affairs of this world organization and has contributed to its peace efforts. In 1967 the Romanian foreign minister Corneliu Manescu was elected president of the United Nations General Assembly for one year—a great honor for a small nation.

The years under the Communist regimes, headed first by Gheorghe Gheorghe-Dej and then Nicolae Ceausescu took their toll in Romania. Harsh oppression denied the citizens the right of free speech and dissent. Large amounts of the agricultural output of the country were exported for monetary gain while in Romania there were long bread lines, empty store shelves, and the Romanian people starved.

In 1989 a demonstration that began in the city of Timisoara quickly spread throughout the country. In a violent and quick revolution the Communist regime was overthrown. Ceausescu was arrested, tried, and executed all within a few days. Ion Iliescu was elected president in the first free multiparty election.

# 6

# The Historic Regions of Romania

In 1947, when Romania was declared a republic, it was officially named the Romanian People's Republic. In 1965 when a new constitution became the law of the land, the country's name became The Socialist Republic of Romania. The name was altered to show that the entire country had changed over to the socialist system of government and public ownership. Today, after the overthrow of communism, it is simply called Romania. The country's flag has also changed back to its three bands of blue, yellow, and red without the emblem put on it by the communist regime.

After the revolution of 1989, a new constitution was written and ratified. The head of state is the president elected by popular vote. The president appoints the prime minister who serves as the head of the government. The prime minister in turn appoints the Council of Ministers, who serve as his advisers. The president is the commander of the armed forces and represents the country in

**A vineyard in Transylvania.**

foreign affairs. The prime minister administers the government and its domestic and foreign policies.

The legislative branch is a two-house parliament. The Senate has 143 seats and the Chamber of Deputies has 343 seats. Both of their members are elected by for four-year terms.

There are 41 counties that administer their own local affairs. Historically Romania is divided into eight regions. Although these regions perform no administrative functions, they are important because they have a long history and form regional boundaries. You can always tell from which region a Romanian comes by the way he speaks and dresses.

Let us look at the eight regions in turn. Beginning in the north,

**A common sight in the Romanian countryside—regional costumes and horse-drawn cart.**

there is the region of Maramures, which borders on the Ukraine. This region is small in size and population. Its inhabitants are mostly farmers and woodcutters. The country here is hilly and mountainous. The main town is Baia Mare with a population of over 148,000. Baia Mare has chemical works and mills that process silver, lead and other metal ores from the nearby mines.

South of Maramures is Transylvania. This is the largest of Romania's regions. Its inhabitants are of Romanian, Hungarian, and German descent. You may know the poem about the Pied Piper of Hamelin. An old legend says that the Germans living in Transylvania are the descendants of the children who followed the Pied Piper into the cave after he had rid the city of rats. When they came out of the cave they found themselves in Transylvania

46

and settled down there! There are large farms and vineyards in Transylvania; and there are forest-clad mountains where coal is mined.

The region of Crisana lies west of Transylvania and borders on Hungary. The people of Crisana, who are of Romanian and Hungarian descent, are great farmers. The fertile plains and hills of Crisana produce grains, sugar beet, vegetables and fruit. The farmers also keep large herds of dairy cattle and flocks of geese. Silver, lead, and copper are mined in the hills, and some of the best marble and granite in the country are quarried here. This region is also famous for its mineral springs.

Although Crisana is heavily populated, most of its towns lie in the plains on the banks of the rivers. The main town is Oradea with a population of 220,850. Oradea has become a major industrial center with shoe and furniture factories, flour mills, glass works and an aluminum plant.

The province of Banat lies in southwest Romania on the borders of Yugoslavia. In the south, Banat borders on the Danube. The population are of mixed Romanian and Serb stock, most of whom live in large villages on the plains.

Wheat, barley, and corn are cultivated in the plains. The south of the region, which is mountainous, is an important center of the Romanian iron and steel industry because of the coal and iron-ore deposits. The main town of Banat is Timisoara with a population of 333,360.

The region of Oltenia lies south of the Carpathian Mountains between the Danube and Olt rivers. It has broad valleys, hills,

A view of the harbor at Constanta, Romania's most important Black Sea port.

and mountains. The people of this region are famous for their national costume. The women wear red skirts, and white blouses embroidered in red. The men's costume is a long white shirt and trousers, a black tunic, and a red sash.

Corn, wheat, and tobacco are cultivated in the valleys, and there are vineyards and plum orchards in the hills. The main town in Oltenia is Craiova with a population of 275,000. Craiova was once a Roman town called Nova Castra. Today it is an important industrial center based on heavy engineering.

If we travel east from Oltenia across the Olt River, we come to Mutenia, or the Land of the Mountains, the third largest of the regions. Muntenia is bordered by the Carpathian Mountains to the north and the Danube to the south and east. The mountains here are famous because of the black goats, bears, and deer which roam over them, and because of the scenery, which is spectacular.

In spite of its name, Muntenia has wide rolling plains in the south. The people work on the land or in the oil fields and refineries. Wheat, corn, tobacco, and sunflowers are the main crops. Large herds of dairy cattle and pigs are reared here also.

The people of Muntenia are very religious. They have built many beautiful churches and monasteries among the wooded hills. In this part of Romania there are wayside shrines where the peasants stop to pray. The main town of the province is the capital city of Bucharest, with a population of 2,300,000.

The region of Dobrudja lies east of Muntenia across the Danube. It is Romania's only maritime region. The population is a mixture of Romanians, Tartars, and Turks, who make a living from fishing and farming, and from catering for tourists at the seaside resorts. The main town of Dobrudja is Constanta, with a population of 350,000. Constanta is not only an industrial town but also Romania's most important port on the Black Sea coast.

The map shows us that Moldavia, Romania's second largest region, is bounded by the Prut River and Moldova to the east and by the Carpathian Mountains to the west. The emblem of the region is the head of an aurochs surmounted by a star. (The aurochs is a wild ox that was hunted to extinction a few centuries ago.) In the north of the region are the ruins of many medieval forts and monasteries. There are also many churches famous for the paintings on their outer walls.

The Moldavian people emigrated to their present lands many

centuries ago from the regions of Transylvania and Maramures. Moldavia is called after the Moldova River. A Romanian prince named the river after his favorite dog, Moldova, who was drowned there during a hunt.

Moldavia has a varied landscape of mountains, hills and plains. Valuable forests of soft timber cover the mountainsides. In the valleys there are oil fields. Orchards and vineyards have been planted on the hills, while the main produce of the plains is grains and sugar beet. The principal town of the province is Iasi with a population of over 344,000. Iasi has chemical factories and engineering works.

# 7

# Transportation and Travel

Romania is a meeting place for trade routes linking western Europe with the countries of the Orient and the Middle East. This means that much of the flow of trade between East and West, called "transit trade," is carried by Romanian roads, waterways, and railways. This trade brings substantial income to the country.

There are over 7,500 miles (12,069 kilometers) of railway line in Romania. The lines have been built in two great circles. One of these circles links the major cities on the Transylvanian Plateau. The other circle links the cities in the plains surrounding the mountains. The two circles are linked by numerous branches that cross the mountains through valleys and tunnels.

Bucharest is Romania's most important railway center. Railway lines connect Bucharest with most of Europe's capitals as far away as Paris in the west and Moscow in the east.

Many Romanian trains still use steam engines, although more and more are changing over to diesels, which are faster and more economical. In the mountains where gradients are steep,

**A railway bridge across the Danube.**

Romanian engineers have built narrow-gauge tracks. About one-fourth of the lines are electrified.

There is a good network of main roads in Romania but only about half of all the roads are paved. Some secondary roads have only a covering of loose stones. Heaps of stones are placed by the roadside so that maintenance workers can fill up potholes. If you drive through the plains, you will find that the road runs straight on for long distances. But the mountain roads are narrow and steep, with hairpin bends, and the smallest mistake can send a car plunging over a precipice.

Although Romania has many rivers, it has few waterways. Romania's rivers have a fast and variable rate of flow which, except for the Danube, makes them unsuitable for navigation. But oceangoing cargo boats can sail up the Danube from the Black Sea as far as the Romanian ports of Galati and Braila. Boats from the Ukraine and Russia laden with iron ore and coke, or from Lebanon and Egypt laden with oranges, lemons, and bales of cotton, dock at these ports to unload their cargoes. In exchange they load grain, timber, hides, and foodstuffs. Beyond these two ports, smaller rivercraft are used for navigation. Barges, some of which are self-propelled, make their way up the Danube carrying oil, timber, grains, and other bulky goods. The barges return from Upper Danube countries such as Germany and Austria laden with steel girders, cars, machinery, and other manufactured goods.

All of Romania's major cities have an airport and are linked by air routes. The national airline company, Tarom, controls all air traffic. Air travel within Romania is cheap and competes with

**Straight, tree-lined roads like this one are typical of the Romanian plains.**

**A view of the airport near Bucharest.**

train travel. Tarom flies mostly Russian-made airliners and cargo planes, but the company also uses British and American planes on international routes. Modern Romanian airliners now carry many tourists and provide every kind of luxury for their passengers. Tarom has planes flying to and from Europe, Africa, Asia, and Latin America.

# 8

# Forests and Fisheries

Romania is a land of vast forests. Except in the plains and on the high mountains where it is too cold and rocky for trees to grow, forests cover much of the country. In fact, about 30 percent of it is forest land. Every year many trees are felled for building, industry and the export trade. As the trees are cut down, new ones are planted to protect the land from soil erosion and to prevent landslides.

The forests of northern Romania are the best in the country. The silver fir and spruce fir grow here. The wood of the spruce fir is especially suitable for musical instruments such as violins and for boats and gliders. On the mountain slopes of Transylvania and Moldavia, there are huge forests of silver fir, larch, and pine. The timber that is felled here is used for building and for making furniture and paper.

Further south, on the hills and in the valleys, there are great forests of beech and oak that produce high-quality timber. Hard beech wood is used for building and furniture. Oak is used for making barrels, flooring, and railway sleepers.

There are also small forests of walnut trees in the far south of the country where the climate is warm. Walnut wood has a beautiful grain and can be polished, so the best logs are cut into very thin sheets of wood that are used for veneering. (Veneering is overlaying a cheaper wood with a thin sheet of a more expensive one.)

Cut timber is hauled from the forests either by tractors or, where the ground is rough and steep, by teams of oxen. The logs are loaded onto railway wagons for delivery to saw mills or for export. In remote mountain districts where there are no roads or railways, the logs are sometimes carried by overhead cable across cliffs and narrow valleys. But the easiest way to transport logs is to float them down streams and rivers. Sometimes wooden troughs, or timber slides, are built in the stream. They may run for some distance, carrying the logs to a main river or lake. Here, timber haulers lash the logs together into rafts that are then steered down to the timber mill or railway head. On lakes, where there is no current, tugs are used to haul the logs.

During the long summer months the trees grow and are full of sap. So the Romanian lumbermen work through the winter and early spring when the wood is dry, and in the summer they find other work. Some work in the mines or on farms. Others become rangers and patrol the forests. They examine the trees for disease and insect pests, and keep a lookout from their watchtowers for any outbreaks of fire, which can devastate forests in a matter of hours. The forest rangers also see that the firebreaks that crisscross the forest (to prevent any fire which does break out from spreading) are kept clear of trees and bushes.

**Logs on the lake above the Bicaz Dam.**

The many streams and rivers of Romania are rich with fish. Trout and salmon are caught in mountain streams. Carp, roach, perch, and eels are caught all along the banks of the Danube and in its tributary rivers in the plains. Romania's most important fishing region is the Danube delta, famous for its great variety of fish, which range from carp, roach, and bream to the valuable sterlet and sturgeon. Caviar, the black roe of the sturgeon, is extracted from the fish when still alive and is either canned on the spot or rushed to the factories for packing. The sturgeon itself is filleted and smoked, or tinned in tomato sauce or a wine sauce.

Fishermen also catch crayfish and frogs that live in the marshes. The two species of edible frog that are found here are called *Rana esculenta* and *Rana ridibunda*. Only the legs are eaten. They taste like lobster, and are regarded as a great delicacy.

57

Deep-sea fishing is impossible in the Black Sea because of the toxic gases at the bottom that destroy all vegetation and other forms of life. The toxic gases arise because of the absence of deep currents and the lack of ventilation. The only place where fishing is possible is along the coast where the water is shallow and where there are surface currents. Fishermen catch red and grey mullet and herrings there.

# 9

# Industry, Oil, and Mines

In spite of great natural resources, Romania was a nation of peasant farmers at the beginning of the 20th century. The many years of warfare against the Turks had prevented the industrial development of the country. Clothes, carpets, and many household goods were made at home or by craftsmen in small workshops. Manufactured goods were imported from abroad in exchange for wheat, fruit, wines, and various raw materials.

The first factories to be built in Romania were set up with the help of private companies from Britain, France, and other industrial nations. These companies provided machinery, engineers, and money. They sometimes owned the new factories, or shared the ownership with the Romanian State.

At that time, the Romanians had no idea that their country was rich in mineral oil. The people used to draw oil from shallow

**An oil refinery in the Danube plain.**

wells or from seepages and use it for fuel or for oiling their carts. Crude oil was also used for healing wounds and sores on both human beings and beasts of burden. Little did they suspect what wealth they had! At last companies from Britain and America were asked by the Romanians to prospect for oil. These companies discovered millions of gallons of it under the Danube plain. They dug deep oil wells and built huge refineries and storage tanks, laying the foundations of Romania's modern oil industry.

The Second World War and Romania's occupation by the Russian army put an end to the help and money the country was receiving from the West. After that Romania had to develop its industries with help from the Soviet Union and other Communist countries. The whole economy was based on government planning, and factories had to fulfil the production targets that were set for them. As in the Soviet Union, there were several Five-Year Plans (so called because they provided a plan of economic development over a five-year period) for the development of Romanian heavy industry and electric power.

The west of the country is more industrialized than the east. In

**A view of Hunedoara at night. This town now has a sizeable population many of whom work at the iron and steel plants.**

Transylvania there are important mines where coal and salt, as well as iron-ore, copper, lead, and other useful metals are extracted. Important iron and steel plants have been built at Hunedoara in the southwest of the province near coking coal deposits. There are also large iron and steel works at Resita in the region of Banat. The iron and steel made here are used for railways, pipelines, girders, and heavy engineering products.

Transylvania is rich in natural gas. Wells are dug deep in the earth to reach the deposits. Then the gas is carried through pipelines to industrial towns. A long pipeline carries gas across the mountains from Transylvania to Bucharest. Natural gas has other uses besides being a valuable source of heat. Chemical factories in Bucharest use it for making chemical fertilizers, plastics, and synthetic rubber.

We have learned how mineral oil was discovered. Today it is one of Romania's most important industries. There are two large oil fields in Romania: one in the Danube Plain and one in the valleys of central Moldavia. The deepest oil wells are in the Danube Plain and are 1,500 feet below ground. The oil is carried through pipelines to the refineries at Ploesti and Cimpina. The oil field in Moldavia is not so large as the one in the Danube Plain. But it has two important refineries, as well as chemical factories that use oil for making medicines, synthetic fibers, dyes, bitumen, and other products.

Romania was once the second largest producer of crude oil in Europe after the former Soviet Union. Its reserves of oil have been depleting though and no longer meet the needs of its own

**The huge concrete dam at the Bicaz hydroelectric power station.**

people and industries. Romania started extracting oil from the Black Sea in the late 1980s to try to increase its supply.

Romanian factories and transportation services do not rely entirely on oil as a source of power. The generation of cheap hydroelectric power has been given top priority by the Romanian government since the end of the Second World War. At Bicaz, in the mountains of Moldavia, Romanian engineers have built a huge concrete dam. This dam holds the water of the Bistrita River in a very deep artificial lake several miles long. The water from the new lake shoots down a series of man-made waterfalls and releases enough energy to work the generators at the main power station and at 12 smaller power stations lower down the river. Here there are cement works, paper factories, and textile mills that use large amounts of electricity.

Another dam and power station has been built across the

Danube at the Iron Gates Rapids. The Iron Gates Power Station is owned jointly by Romania and Serbia. The two countries not only share the electricity produced but also benefit from the improved navigation on the Danube because of the long artificial lake behind the dam. A road now runs along the top of the dam, making traffic easier between the two countries.

Now let us pay a visit to the industrial region in southeastern Romania. This region is centered on two important ports on the lower reaches of the Danube—Galati and Braila. In the past Galati and Braila were busy commercial ports on the Danube handling grain and timber. But the two ports have grown rapidly and many new industries have been introduced on their outskirts. Huge modern iron and steel works have been built at enormous cost. The iron and steel are used by shipbuilding and repair yards where tugs, barges, and cargo boats of over 12,000 tons are built. In addition to the shipyards there are machine tool factories, engineering works, paper mills, and chemical plants.

Romania's economy was greatly mishandled under the

**A view of the center of Gulati, a busy port on the Danube.**

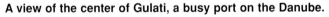

Communist regimes. Because of the heavy emphasis on industrialization and the exporting of a large portion of its agricultural products, Romania's economy slowly declined. Today Romania is one of the poorest countries in Europe struggling to repair the damage that was done.

# 10

# Farms and Crops

In spite of the fact that Romania became an industrial nation, about 35 percent of its people are still employed in farming. Farms in Romania do not produce enough food for the country's population so some of the food supply has to be imported. They do supply many manufacturing industries with raw materials such as hides for the production of leather goods, and fruit and vegetables for canning.

Before the Second World War most farms in Romania were smallholdings belonging to peasants. There were only a few large farms belonging either to landowners, or to the state where they were used for improving crops and for other research. In 1949 the government decided to set up collective farms by joining the smallholdings of the peasants together, and nationalizing the large farms. At first the peasants were resentful and even refused to work on the new farms. But gradually they learned to use modern methods, and found that better crops and healthy livestock meant more money. By 1962 most of the land in the country was

**A typical Romanian farm.**

being farmed by the collective system and hardly anybody owned private land any more. After 1989 the larger collective farms were broken up into individual peasant holdings. Some of the smaller farmers have formed associations to help each other develop their farms.

There are machine and tractor stations (which we will call M.T.S. for short) in Romania. Each M.T.S. has a supply of tractors and other farm machinery, as well as repair workshops. The stations are manned by trained agricultural engineers, who drive the tractors and handle the machinery. Whenever a farm has a job to do that involves the use of a tractor or some other piece of farm machinery, it sends a request to its local M.T.S. The M.T.S. serves the farm and charges a fee. In this way the farms are not obliged to invest money in expensive machinery. They can use any surplus money they earn for improving the land and increasing production.

Farms in Romania are allowed to choose the kind of crops they will grow, or the stock they will rear. There are some farms that

66

grow only grains and some that grow fruit or rear poultry and pigs. Others build greenhouses in which they grow tomatoes, asparagus, and early vegetables. Farmers often erect wooden frames in their fields and cover them with transparent plastic sheets to trap the heat and protect the plants from frost. In this way they grow large quantities of vegetables.

Romania is a major producer of corn and wheat. Corn is perhaps the most important single crop because it provides the staple food of the peasants. The corn is ground into a fine powder that is used for making a porridge called *mamaliga*. Corn flour can also be used for baking into a heavy bread called *turta*. In industry corn is used for making starch, glucose, and alcohol. The stems and leaves of the corn plant are used as fodder for cattle.

Romania produces large quantities of barley, oats, rye, sunflowers, sugar beet, and potatoes. The plains and hills provide most of the grain crops, though oats and rye grow well in mountain valleys.

Farmers who live in low-lying areas of the Danube Plain rear livestock. The land is often marshy and no grain crops can be grown. But there are many meadows, where dairy cattle graze. They have been bred from prize cattle brought to Romania from

**Girls in hand-embroidered traditional dress picking grapes in one of Romania's many vineyards.**

**A cattle market.**

Switzerland and Britain. The larger farms also rear buffaloes, which were introduced from India. The buffaloes are jet black and have curved flat horns. They are gentle animals that like to wallow in muddy ponds. But they are also very strong and are used for pulling heavy carts. The buffalo cow gives rich milk from which a creamy cheese is made.

The hot summers and plentiful supply of water in the irrigated Danube Plain make the area suitable for growing rice and cotton. The Romanian government encouraged the cultivation of these two crops because all the country's rice and cotton was imported from abroad.

Flax and hemp are grown in northern Moldavia and Dobrudja

68

where the climate is dry. These plants are grown mainly for the textile industry. The silky fibers of the flax and hemp stems can be spun and woven into cloth. Hemp fibers are stronger and thicker than flax and are used for making coarse cloth and string, rope and sacking. The seeds of both flax and hemp are rich in oil. The oil is pressed from the seed and is used for mixing with paints.

The hills of Transylvania and Moldavia have good soil for vine-growing, and there are vineyards on many of the slopes. The bulk of the grape crop is used for making wine and brandy. Romania is one of the top wine-producing countries of Europe. Large quantities of Romanian red and white wines are exported to many countries of the world.

Tobacco is a major cash crop. It is grown on a large scale in the Danube Plain. The farms growing tobacco have to sell their whole crop to the state tobacco company which owns factories for making cigarettes.

One of Romania's most beautiful crops is the poppy. Cultivated poppy fields lie pink and red beneath the summer sun. Later the

**Getting in the harvest.**

green pods are collected and the white juice from the unripe seed is extracted for making morphine and other valuable drugs used by doctors all over the world. Some poppy seeds are left to ripen and are used for sprinkling on bread or buns or as a filling for cakes.

There are mulberry groves in many parts of the country. The black and white berries of the mulberry tree are used for making jam. The mulberry leaves are fed to silkworms, which make the cocoons from which natural silk is obtained. The silk is then spun by hand, with the aid of a distaff.

Plums grow well in Romania because of the long, hot summers. Plum orchards produce large yellow or purple plums. Some are eaten as fresh fruit. Others are picked and stored in vats where they are left to ferment. When the sugary juice in the plum ferments, it changes into alcohol. After fermentation the pulp is distilled and turned into a strong brandy called *tuica*, the national drink of Romania.

Bees have been kept in Romania since ancient times. Romanian children learn at school that when the Romans conquered Dacia they found many hives in the country. Today there are many farms (or apiaries) specializing in beekeeping. These farms are situated in the west and in the hills of southern Romania. They supply honey, and wax for candles, polish, and tanning. Jars of Romanian honey are exported to Britain and other countries.

The greatest worry of Romanian farmers is rain. Too much rain swells the waters of the Danube and its tributaries—especially in the spring—causing floods. Crops are destroyed, bridges swept away, and livestock drowned. On the other hand, too little rain when crops are growing means a poor harvest and hardship for the peasants.

There are special farms in Romania where trained scientists called agronomists study the problems of farming. They write magazines and books for peasants on how to deal with pests and plant diseases. Weevils, beetles, and rats cause much damage to grain crops in Romania. Plant diseases like blight, or pests like the Colorado beetle, can spoil the potato crop. But modern insecticides are helping to protect crops. Scientists are also testing and experimenting with improved strains of wheat, corn, and other grains. Already they have succeeded in finding a more productive variety of corn, which means that farmers can grow more corn in each field.

# 11

# Cities, Towns, and Spas

Many Romanians, like their ancestors, prefer to live in cities and towns. More and more people have moved away from their villages and hamlets to the cities, where they can work in factories and earn high wages. So Romanian towns are growing rapidly. Tall blocks of apartments have had to be built on their outskirts to house the new population.

Romanian townsfolk are sociable and can often be seen chatting in the street or sitting on their front doorsteps. On warm summer evenings, whole families stroll up and down the main street, stopping for a drink at a beer garden or café.

Many Romanian towns are strategically placed at crossroads, on hilltops, or in sheltered valleys. Let us pay a visit to a few of these towns. The first is called Turnu-Severin, and it is Romania's most ancient Roman city. It lies on a hill on the left bank of the Danube River, a short distance from the Iron Gates Rapids. We have learned that it was an important garrison town under the Romans, who built a bridge there across the river. You can still see the ruins of Roman villas and some fine mosaic floors that are carefully preserved in a park.

Today Turnu-Severin is a city of broad streets, shady avenues and large squares suitable for modern traffic. Its mills and factories are supplied with electricity from the giant power station at the Iron Gates. Turnu-Severin has a wide harbor for the tugs and barges of the Danube and extensive shipbuilding and repair yards. Passenger steamers carrying tourists from Belgrade and Vienna call at Turnu-Severin. The visitors tour the city and have a meal in one of its many restaurants.

Craiova, the capital of Dolj county, lies in the middle of a plain in southwestern Romania. The city has a long and unfortunate history (like Turnu-Severin, it dates back to Roman times). In the Middle Ages it was plundered and partly destroyed by the Turks. Then in 1790 there was a major earthquake that made half the population homeless; and this disaster was followed, a few years later, by the plague. In spite of its tragic past, Craiova grew in size and population. Today it is a large industrial city and an important railway center. There is a university in addition to various technical schools and colleges. In the city center there are modern shops, hotels, and restaurants.

Bucharest, the most beautiful city in Romania, lies on the banks of the Dimbovita River in the middle of the Danube Plain. There was a settlement here in prehistoric times. Later it became a meeting point of busy trade routes and a central market for pigs, poultry, wheat and other produce of the plains. During the Middle

Ages a fort was built at Bucharest to protect the population from Turkish marauders.

Today there is little left of the old city. As more and more Romanians settled in Bucharest, the city expanded rapidly in all directions. Now Bucharest is the largest city in southeastern Europe. Because it had wide boulevards, smart shops, beautiful gardens, and fountains, Bucharest was once nicknamed the Paris of the East. Due to a very destructive earthquake in 1977 and many decades of neglect, its former beauty has faded.

Bucharest is not only an industrial and commercial center. It is also the center of Romania's administrative and cultural life. The parliament and government have their offices there. The Romanian Academy, which was founded in 1879 and is famous for its scientists, scholars, and artists, is in Bucharest. The city also contains museums with valuable art collections and many

**A square in the capital city of Bucharest.**

**One of Bucharest's many churches. The Patriarch of the Orthodox Church has his palace in the capital.**

ancient churches. The Patriarch—the head of the Romanian Orthodox Church—has his house on top of a hill surrounded by gardens and churches.

Now let us visit the region of Transylvania, where there are cities that are very similar to those of southern Germany or Austria. Here we will find Romanian, German, and Hungarian communities existing side by side.

Brasov is situated in the southeastern corner of Transylvania. It is one of Romania's largest cities with a population of 351,000. The city is set in beautiful surroundings—on all sides there are mountains and thick forests of fir and pine. Brasov is often called the most German city in Romania. Its population is made up of Germans and Romanians. The old town hall and cathedral are built in the Gothic style, under the German influence.

Cluj-Napoca, too, is situated near mountains. It has a Roman Catholic cathedral that was built in the 14th century. But the city itself dates back to Roman times, when it was an important garrison town defending the approaches to northern Transylvania. Today Cluj-Napoca has a large Hungarian population as well as Romanian and German communities, numbering 290,000 in all. There is a university for Hungarian and Romanian students and there are various technical schools. In the center of the city are smart hotels and restaurants.

Cluj-Napoca is one of the most important industrial centers of Romania, with textile mills, and factories manufacturing shoes, porcelain, cigarettes, and matches.

Arad lies on the banks of the Mures River in western Romania. It is surrounded by plains. The countryside is rich in corn fields, tobacco plantations, and vineyards.

Today Arad has a population of 182,000, mostly of Hungarian and Romanian descent. It is an important road and railway junction. One of the largest railway factories in Romania is situated at Arad. There are also machine-tool works, textile mills, breweries, and food-canning factories.

Now let us pay a visit to Timisoara Banat region. The city is founded on the site of an old fortress, situated on a small plain. It is linked by canal to the Danube, which is just across the border in Serbia.

Timisoara has a university and a beautiful Orthodox cathedral. The town is expanding rapidly and new housing estates have recently been built. One of the largest chemical works in Romania is at Timisoara. There are also flour mills and shoe factories. Timisoara was the site of demonstrations in December of 1989 that started the revolution that toppled the Communist dictatorship of Nicolae Ceausescu.

Let us end our visit to Romania's towns by reading about two famous spas that date from Roman times.

Baile Felix ("felix" meaning "happy" in Latin) lies in a sheltered valley in the region of Crisana. Because of its hot springs, even in winter the ground never freezes. Steaming hot water, rich in minerals, rises from the springs, filling two large swimming pools and many baths, and running into several ponds where the lotus and the water lily bloom. Banana trees and Chinese rose bushes grow in nearby gardens, helped by the warmth from the ponds. People suffering from rheumatism and other illnesses come to Baile Felix in order to rest and to receive medical treatment. The Baths are so popular and crowded that many new villas and sanatoria have been built.

Baile Herculane (or Hercules' baths) lies in a narrow valley in the mountains of Banat province. This spa was popular in Roman times, when it was used by Roman officers and soldiers. It is named after the Temple of Hercules built there by the Romans. An aqueduct connects the temple with the hot springs that gush from the mountainside.

Today, Baile Herculane is a resort with smart tourist hotels, restaurants, and public gardens, as well as comfortable hospitals for sick people who visit the baths for medical treatment.

# 12

# Country Life

In order to see a little of what country life is like in Romania, let us explore a village in the hills of Oltenia in the south. The village lies in a valley on the edge of a gully. After heavy rain a torrent rushes wildly down the gully; but in hot weather it dwindles to a trickle. The villagers have planted trees and bushes on the upper slopes of the hillsides to stop heavy rainwater from washing the earth down into the village.

Gnarled mulberry trees line the unpaved road which winds up to the village. There are timber-built houses on either side of the main street, their walls plastered and whitewashed, their pointed roofs covered with shingles (small rectangular pieces of flat wood). Other roofs are covered with overlapping sheets of zinc, painted red or green. Each house has a small flower garden in front and a farmyard and vegetable garden at the back. In the middle of the village is a new building; it is made of concrete and has a tiled roof. This is the town hall. Across the street from the town hall is a long building with a flat roof. Over the entrance is

**A timber-built house with a shingle roof.**

a notice board bearing the sign *Scoala Generala,* which means "General School." Further down is the village store and next to it is an inn with a beer garden.

Most of the houses in the village have a ground floor and a top story. The ground floor consists merely of a cellar and storerooms. To reach the first story—and the front door—you mount steep steps to a balcony surrounded by climbing vines. Beyond are the living quarters, consisting of a large living room, bedroom, and kitchen.

The Romanians keep their houses clean and cool in summer. They have brightly colored carpets and mats on the floor and hanging on the walls. The furniture is handmade and simple. The living room has a large table with stools or chairs around it and a cupboard in a corner. The bedroom has two large beds—the parents sleep in one, the children in the other. There is no running water in the house and no inside toilet.

At the back of the house are a few apricot and plum trees and a

**Romanian crafts and skills are often devoted to producing furniture, carpets, and pottery for the home.**

vegetable garden. The villagers grow their own vegetables including tomatoes, pumpkins, and cucumbers, and green peppers that are delicious when filled with rice and cooked in a thick sauce. Some villagers keep a cow or a goat. Because it is hot and there are no refrigerators, most of the milk is used for making cheese or yogurt.

Hens and pigs roam freely about the farmyard. In one corner there is a barn for storing corn cobs. Next to the barn is the pigsty and henhouse. Farm carts and implements are kept in a shed at the bottom of the yard.

Most of the villagers, men and women alike, work on the farms. The men do the rough, hard work in the fields while the women prepare food, milk the cows, and collect eggs. The women work very long hours, for as well as working on the farm they clean their houses, prepare pickles, and make their own jams for the winter.

Romanian peasant children are expected to work during their

summer holidays. They help with the harvest, and they look after the cattle and sheep which graze the stubble after the wheat has been cut. They have to make sure that the animals do not stray, for the fields are wide open and have no hedges or fences.

The village blacksmith is a gypsy. He shoes the horses and oxen. He repairs cauldrons, pots and pans, and makes ornaments of metal. On Sunday the gypsy turns musician. He plays the fiddle for customers at the village inn or at private celebrations.

The village priest is an important man. The peasants come to him for advice. His church is on the edge of the village. Every Sunday the church is packed with worshipers; they light candles to the saint at the local shrine as a token of their respect. St Mary's day, in the middle of August, is just one of the many religious festivals that they honor. The peasants also ask the priest to hold special services in memory of their dead and to bless any sick relations. When there is drought the priest is asked to pray for rain.

Romanian peasants are hospitable; even strangers or foreigners are made welcome and are invited to stay for as long as they like. On arrival, guests are offered rose-petal jam or green nuts preserved in syrup, which they eat off glass plates no larger than coffee saucers. The jam is served with a glass of cold water to take away the sweetness. Then the guests are offered Turkish coffee, which is bittersweet and strong. The black coffee is drunk out of small cups twice the size of a thimble.

From Oltenia let us travel to the Black Sea coast and visit a village in there. The coast is flat with long, sandy beaches. The land here is crisscrossed with lagoons and narrow channels, where the many branches of the Danube River meander on the last lap of their journey to the Black Sea. The banks are covered with thick reeds and rushes.

The village is situated on high ground a few miles inland. One or two pine trees grow in the poor, sandy soil. The village has wide streets and small square houses built of bricks. The bricks are made of mud mixed with reeds or straw and dried in the sun. The flattish roofs are covered with reeds laid over thick rafters. The walls of the houses are whitewashed. The windows are small with shutters painted green or red. At the back of each house is a long shed where the family boat is kept. There are no hedges or fences; instead, tall sunflowers or corn plants grow outside the house or along the garden borders.

The villagers are a mixture of Romanians and Russians who fled from their country because of religious persecution. The men wear blue cotton tunics and trousers, rubber boots and straw hats. Some of the older ones have long beards. The women wear black dresses and black head scarves.

Most of the families, but not all, make a living by fishing in the Danube delta or along the coast. But nowadays more and more of them work as reed cutters in the swamps of the delta. The reeds fetch high prices at the pulping factories where they are turned into cellulose for making paper and even artificial silk. Reeds are also needed in the village for fuel and for thatching. Some villagers are skilled guides for visiting tourists, showing them the wild life and natural scenery of the area.

Now let us move on to northern Romania and read about a village in a valley of the Carpathian Mountains. Here are thick forests of silver fir and spruce. Higher up the mountainside are Alpine pastures where shepherds with dogs guard the flocks of sheep and goats.

The village is a cluster of log cabins and chalets on the banks of a rushing stream. Higher up, the stream is dammed to supply energy for a flour mill. Each chalet has low walls but a very high and pointed roof. The roof is made of shingles that are arranged in overlapping rows like the scales of a fish. The church is made of timber in the same way as the houses. It has a tall and slender spire.

Each house has a large room that is kept for guests. There are

**A village square.**

rugs and mats and embroidered woolen cushions on the floor. The walls are decorated with beautiful napkins, and with goblets and plates that have flowers painted on them. There are also racks in which carved wooden spoons and spindles are kept.

The villagers are famous for their dress. The men wear long white shirts, trousers, and colored tunics. The women wear white skirts with flounces around the hem, and fine blouses embroidered with red flowers. They braid their hair into pigtails and wear necklaces of silver or gold coins.

The people in this part of Romania are very industrious and have a high standard of living. They grow wheat, corn, fruit, such as apples and pears, and walnuts. They keep cattle and sheep. The women weave carpets, aprons, and rugs on handlooms. Some of the men are woodcutters or carpenters. Others work in mines where copper, zinc, silver or uranium is extracted. Work in the uranium mines is dangerous because of radioactivity, and the miners wear special suits of lead as a protection.

# 13

# Schools and Sports

About 50 years ago, many Romanians over the age of 14 were illiterate. They were unable to read or write. They had missed school when they were young or had been unable to go to school because of the war. So the government set up special evening courses all over the country to teach illiterate people how to read, write and do easy sums. These courses were so successful that by 1955 there were hardly any illiterate people left in the country.

**Romanian schoolchildren.**

Today all schools in Romania are free except for a few private universities. Boys and girls in towns and villages begin school when they are six. The school they go to is a general school, covering both primary and secondary education. It has eight forms. Attending the general school, or *Scoala Generala*, is compulsory for all.

Uniforms are worn in most schools. Boys wear long blue trousers with short jackets and peaked caps. Instead of a tie they wear a small colored scarf. The girls wear short belted dresses, or skirts and blouses, and long cotton stockings. All of them wear a square piece of cloth, usually red, on their sleeve bearing the name of the school and a registration number.

Children who have completed their general schooling at the age of 16 may either start work or continue their education at a lycée (a word borrowed from the French name for a grammar school) or at a technical school. Before being accepted by these schools, they must pass a competitive examination. The lycée has four forms. The bottom form is called the ninth form because the children have already completed eight years at the *Scoala Generala*. The top form is called the 12th form. In the 11th and 12th forms the pupils are divided into two streams, one specializing in mathematics and science; the other in Latin and literature.

At the end of their four years at the lycée, the pupils take a final examination, called, as in France, a baccalaureate. Pupils who pass their baccalaureate can get jobs in the civil service or in industry. Those who want to go to a university have to take an entrance examination. The successful ones who go to a universi-

**Bucharest University.**

ty are given generous grants. There are many universities in Romania, the largest ones being in Bucharest and Iasi.

Pupils in Romanian schools learn much the same subjects as boys and girls elsewhere. But they learn Latin from an early age. This is because the Romanian language has strong Latin roots, many words being the same in both languages. Scientific subjects and modern languages are considered important. Schools have modern science laboratories and equipment. They also have museums that house collections of rocks, stuffed animals, and archaeological remains. Practical skills such as woodwork, pottery, and metalwork are taught, and there are outings to factories, mines and farms where pupils can see how things are made and how people earn their living.

Some Romanian radio and television stations in Bucharest

broadcasts programs for schools. Many of the school programs are bought from Britain and other western countries and are shown to Romanian children with captions in Romanian.

All Romanian school children belong to the Pioneer Organization, which is similar to the boy scout or girl scout movement. Romanian Pioneers are encouraged to help their neighbors and serve the community. They learn first-aid and other useful skills. Pioneers have their own newspaper and run their own holiday camps.

We have learned that the Romanian population is composed of different nationalities. Pupils belonging to these different nationalities receive instruction in their own language, but all must learn Romanian. Textbooks in German, Hungarian, and other languages are sent to the schools needing them.

Schools in Romania close at the beginning of June for the summer holidays, which last until the middle of September. During the long summer months some boys and girls go to camps in the mountains or by the sea. Older pupils go to camps in Serbia, Bulgaria or Russia, while some students prefer to work at home and earn money. They can choose to work on building sites, roads, or farms. Through doing manual work, young people are thought to gain a better understanding of life.

Except in the mountains, where the weather is rainy and cool, Romania has long, dry summers. This means that boys and girls can swim in the rivers and lakes. Swimming is popular in Romania, and many towns and vacation resorts have swimming pools. Some of the pools have artificial wavemakers to make them resemble the sea. There are also many first-class water polo teams in Romania, who compete with each other in matches.

Soccer and Rugby are popular games. Cycling is another popular sport. Cycle races are organized between various towns. An important annual event is the Cycling Tour of Romania, when all the best sportsmen compete for the coveted Cyclists' Cup.

There are some sports which are not very common in Romania, such as hockey, cricket, and golf are never played. Tennis courts are few and can only be found in the larger cities. There is no car racing in Romania but there are some racetracks for motorcycles. There are also air clubs whose members learn piloting, gliding, and parachute jumping.

Romania's cold and snowy winters mean that young people can skate and ski in the mountains. Chalets and cabins have been built for skiers at many mountain resorts. People living in cities can skate on frozen ponds or ice rinks. Although ordinary hockey is unknown, ice hockey is a popular sport with students.

Romanians often hunt in the marshes along the Danube and in the forests of the delta, where there are flocks of wild duck, geese and snipe. Gun parties also go up in the mountains to shoot wolves, bears, red deer, and woodcock.

The Romanian fishing season starts on May 1st and ends on September 15th. Throughout the season anglers fish for salmon and trout in mountain streams. Those who prefer lowland fishing go to the Danube and the broad rivers of the plains, where they catch dace, barbel, and tench. Many anglers fish in the delta, where the best fish are to be caught. Fishing in the delta can be

**Cyclists at the start of a race.**

uncomfortable. Anglers often get lost in the reeds or in the maze of channels; or they become entangled in a particularly unpleasant plant with long, slimy tentacles. Then there are swarms of mosquitoes and winged ants. Experienced anglers always rub a strong-smelling ointment on their skin to keep the mosquitoes and ants away.

**Skiing at a popular resort.**

# 14

# Churches and Monasteries

The introduction of Christianity into Romania can be traced back to the days when the country was a Roman province. Simple Christian tombs of Roman colonizers and ruins of churches have been found on the site of old settlements. So it was through the Romans that the Romanian people were born into the early Christian Church. In the Middle Ages the Early Christian Church split into East and West—into the Orthodox Eastern Church and the Church of Rome. The Romanians came under the influence of the Orthodox Eastern Church. (The word Orthodox means "true faith.")

In the course of centuries Romanian princes built splendid cathedrals, churches, and monasteries. Medieval carpenters, masons, artists, and architects worked together on these buildings. Many of them took years to complete. Wooden doors and pillars were decorated with elaborate carvings. Artists were brought at enormous cost from Italy and Greece to paint frescoes on the ceilings and walls and to design mosaics for the floors. These frescoes and mosaics illustrated scenes from the life of Jesus Christ and the Apostles. Many of the frescoes were painted on the outside walls of churches, and in spite of sun and rain they still preserve their vivid colors of gold, red, and blue.

Our picture shows the beautiful church at Curtea de Arges, in southern Romania. The Romanian Prince Neagoe Basarab ordered the church to be built at the beginning of the 16th century. According to legend, the mason who built it was called Manole. He came from Constantinople and brought marble and mosaics with him. But the stones he laid during the day crumbled at night. Then Manole had a dream; he dreamed that if he walled his wife in, the stones would stand. He believed the dream, and imprisoned his wife forever within the walls of the church. When the church was finished the prince asked Manole whether he could build an even more beautiful one. Unsuspecting and flattered, Manole replied that he could. The prince, not wishing anyone to have a more beautiful church than his own, ordered that Manole should be killed.

In the Middle Ages many monasteries were built in the hills and in sheltered valleys. Some were even perched high up in the mountains of Moldavia and Wallachia. The monasteries were the only places where people could learn to read and write. The monks were great scholars, and people came to them to be taught.

Monasteries also became places of refuge for terrified villagers whose houses had been set fire to and plundered by marauding Turks. The monks built strong walls and towers around their

**The church at Curtea de Arges.**

churches and cloisters to protect them. Today the monasteries of Romania are famous for their art treasures, and some have been turned into museums. Visitors can see silver book covers and platters with holy designs, goblets and candlesticks of gold, and rich tapestries and embroidered hangings for the altar. But perhaps the most precious of the holy objects are the icons—religious pictures, painted on wood or metal. They hang on walls or are placed on wooden stands. They are great works of art. Orthodox believers light candles and pray in front of them. Some icons are reputed to work miracles and heal sick people, and large crowds of pilgrims line up to worship them.

**The painted western wall of the monastery at Voronet, in Moldavia.**

Today the Romanian Orthodox Church has a great influence on the people. The churches are full on Sundays, and everybody participates in religious festivals. There are also Roman Catholic and Protestant churches in Transylvania for the Hungarian and German communities.

A votive painting inside the Voronet monastery.

The outside of another Moldavian monastery—at Humor—where all four walls are covered with religious paintings.

# 15

# Arts and Festivals

The Romanian people are gifted artists. The peasants, who live away from the noise and bustle of cities, have a rich tradition of folklore—beliefs, customs, and fairy tales that are passed on from generation to generation by word of mouth. Folklore has a strong influence on various arts and crafts. Tools, pottery, clothes, carpets, and ornaments made by the peasants are often decorated with pictures from fairy tales or old legends.

**An example of Romanian folk art: beautifully decorated Easter eggs.**

Folk music and dancing is popular throughout Romania. Traditional Romanian folk music and dances are performed on radio and television, in theaters, restaurants, or in the open air at festivals. The artists and dancers wear colorful national costumes. Professional musicians play violins, drums, and flutes while the dancers twirl, click their heels, and leap in the air. A favorite dance is the *hora*, where the performers hold hands and form a circle around the band of musicians. The best folk dancers give displays on television and in famous theaters all over the world. They are greatly admired and earn a lot of money.

It is the custom to celebrate festive seasons such as Christmas and New Year's Eve with folk music and dancing. People also hire folk dancers and musicians to perform at weddings and christenings, when some of the guests come dressed in their national costumes. The men wear long white shirts with black waistcoats and tight-fitting trousers that date from Dacian days. On their feet

**Dancers in traditional costume.**

**A village band.**

they wear pigskin moccasins. The women have petticoats with flounces around the hem and a double apron—at front and back—that forms a kind of fringed skirt with elaborate designs worked in gold thread. They wear fine blouses and gauze-like silk head scarves.

Another aspect of their tradition is the ancient ritual that the peasants observe at burials. A coin is put in the hand of the dead person to pay the ferryman. This belief comes from Greek mythology where Charon, the ferryman, carries the dead souls across the River Styx into Hades.

98

Modern Romanian artists make pottery of all kinds, including bowls, pitchers, and slender vases for flowers. Some of the pottery has simple patterns that are made with the fingernail. Smoke is used on the famous polished black pottery to get the ebony effect and its gloss is obtained by stone polishing. Woodcarvers make expensive furniture and souvenirs for tourists. They also make ornamental figurines, children's toys, and music boxes. The women are skilled in needlework. They also make lace and weave carpets, curtains and other household fabrics with intricate designs and geometrical patterns. At Easter they paint eggs with traditional patterns of fishes, birds, stars, circles, and crosses.

Romanian artists are famous for the dolls they make. The dolls are made of hair, straw, or rags and vary greatly in appearance. They are dressed in miniature national costumes complete with

**Peasants of the Bacau region.**

**Romanian pottery with simple patterns and traditional glazing.**

beads, ribbons and headwear. Romanian dolls often find their way into public or private collections all over the world.

# 16

# Problems of a Developing Country

We have learned about Romania's mineral resources, its factories, vast forests, and fertile farmlands. We have seen that the transit trade through Romania brings the country some revenue. But most Romanians are still peasants. They have low incomes and few savings compared with people in many other European countries. Theirs is a developing country in need of money, especially hard currency from abroad such as pounds and dollars. In order to earn this money, Romania must increase its exports; so the government is trying to find new markets where it can sell the oil, timber, machinery, and tinned and frozen foods that the country produces.

Building new factories with modern equipment brings its own problems, for one needs skilled workers to run expensive factory machinery. So more and more young people are being sent to technical schools at home and abroad to learn skilled trades.

Another major problem is housing. The good jobs that the fac-

**Romania's towns are growing fast. This is a view of a new housing development in the university town of Iasi.**

tories offer have drawn workers from the countryside into towns, and they need houses. Although new blocks of apartments have been built, there is still a serious shortage of accommodation and public services. It is not unusual for more than one family to share a small apartment or live under crowded conditions.

We have learned that people of several different nationalities live in Romania. The Hungarian community in Transylvania is extremely nationalistic. Most Hungarians are loyal citizens of

Romania but there are a few who want the region of Transylvania to become Hungarian territory again. They do not want to accept that Romania as it is today was born in 1918 through the free choice of the majority of people living within its borders.

In the past Romania was called a satellite country because it was forced to obey all the wishes of the government of the Soviet Union. Russia still has an enormous influence on Romania and on the Romanian way of life. Romania and Russia do substantial trade together in raw materials and manufactured goods.

In the past when Romania was a communist country, it did not always agree with the Soviet Union on either home or foreign policy. In 1964 it started pursuing an independent foreign policy. One of the chief causes of disagreement between Romania and the Soviet Union concerned the development of industry. The Soviet Union wanted Romania to develop only a few industries, and to concentrate on producing raw materials and farm produce. The Romanian government refused to do this because it believed that the country had a better future if all kinds of industry were developed.

When war broke out in the Middle East between Israel and the Arab countries in June 1967, Romania was the only Communist country to support Israel. This attitude annoyed the Russian government. Again, when Russian troops invaded Czechoslovakia in August 1968, the Romanian government courageously condemned the Russian aggression and stood by the Czechoslovak people in their hour of need. The Russian leaders were so angry with Romania on this occasion that they threatened to invade

Romania herself. Few small countries in the world would have defied the Soviet Union at such a time!

In the 1980s Romania signed important trade contracts with the United States, West Germany, Britain, and other western countries. Trade between Romania and the West has been increasing all the time.

Communist China also caused argument between Romania and the Soviet Union. The Chinese government was on bad terms with the Russian leaders. And the Romanians remained neutral in this quarrel, much to the annoyance of the Russians. It took great courage for Romania to be so independent in its foreign policy.

In December 1989, Romania showed its courage again and broke its ties with communism. In a spontaneous revolution the dictatorship of Ceausescu was overthrown. Romania is still fighting the effects of so many years with an oppressive government and changing to a new economy has been difficult. Inflation has been a major problem and reached 155 percent in 1998. Romania is again reaching out to the countries of the West. It has applied for membership in NATO and to become a member of the European Union (EU). But Romania is now free to develop its economy and its government in the way which will benefit the people most.

The Romanians are intensely patriotic. They strongly believe in their right to decide their own fate without outside interference. They also believe in the right of all peoples to be independent and free from foreign intervention.

Though Romania is one of Europe's poorest countries, its people hope for a better future. They are a generous and friendly people, willing to open their hearts and homes to visitors from other countries, and tourism is being encouraged as a means of bringing new revenue into the country. It will also allow other peoples to get to know the Romanian culture and people.

Romania enters the 21st century with serious economic difficulties, an infrastructure that badly needs updating and repair after years of neglect, and a population that needs job training. It also enters the new century with a renewed desire to accomplish its goals, retain its culture and beliefs, and to become a vital part of the international community.

# GLOSSARY

**apiary**    Farm or place where bees are raised

*austru*    Hot south wind that blows over the Romanian plains in the summer

*crivat*    Cold wind that blows south from Siberia in the winter

**folklore**    Beliefs, customs, and fairy tales passed on from generation to generation usually by word of mouth

**icon**    Religious picture painted on small pieces of wood or metal used for worship in the Eastern Catholic religions

**karst**    Irregular limestone region with underground streams and caverns

**plateau**    Extensive, level land area raised above adjacent land on at least one side

**soil erosion**    Ecological problem that occurs when rain water washes away the topsoil due to cutting down of the protective trees

**tuica**    National drink of Romania; a strong brandy made from plums

**steppe**    Flat, treeless plain found in Eastern Europe

# INDEX